Self-
Esteem
AND THE 6-SECOND
SECRET

UPDATED EDITION

Self-Esteem

AND THE 6-SECOND SECRET

UPDATED EDITION

Connie Podesta

CORWIN PRESS, INC.
A Sage Publications Company
Thousand Oaks, California

For information:

Corwin Press, Inc.
A Sage Publications Company
2455 Teller Road
Thousand Oaks, California 91320
E-mail: order@corwinpress.com

Sage Publications Ltd.
6 Bonhill Street
London EC2A 4PU
United Kingdom

Sage Publications India Pvt. Ltd.
M-32 Market
Greater Kailash I
New Delhi 110 048 India

Printed in the United States of America

Library of Congress Cataloging-in-Publication Data

Podesta, Connie.
    Self-esteem and the 6-second secret / by Connie Podesta.—
Updated ed.
        p.   cm.
    ISBN 0-7619-7835-6 (cloth: alk. paper)
    ISBN 0-7619-7836-4 (pbk.: alk. paper)
    1. Self-esteem in children.   2. Child rearing.   I. Title: Self-esteem and
the 6-second secret.   II. Title.
    BF723.S3 P63   2001
    158.1—dc21   00-012743

This book is printed on acid-free paper.

01   02   03   04   05   06   07   7   6   5   4   3   2   1

Acquisitions Editor:	Rachel Livsey
Corwin Editorial Assistant:	Phyllis Cappello
Production Editor:	Diane S. Foster/Nevair Kabakian
Editorial Assistant:	Kathryn Journey
Typesetter/Designer:	Lynn Miyata
Cover Designer:	Tracy E. Miller
Design:	Loreen Creative Services
Illustrations:	Dianne J. Harlan and Ellen Stern

Foreword

Having the responsibility of shaping the lives of today's youth is indeed complex. In my roles as educator, therapist, and parent, I have spent many hours contemplating what steps we need to take to ensure that our children become confident, happy adults.

I have read many books on self-esteem that tell us the obvious: Praise children and avoid harsh criticism, and I have attempted to do this with my own children, students, and clients. I have also encouraged and worked with parents to develop skills such as active listening, behavior modifications, using natural consequences, and positive reinforcement. Yet even with these tools, I was still seeing children, including at times my own, who lacked the confidence needed to accomplish their goals.

Connie Podesta's book, *Self-Esteem and the 6-Second Secret,* has allowed me the opportunity to look at self-esteem from a different point of view. For the first time, I understand that many of the things we say or do that we believe to be positive may, in fact, be interpreted as negative. I also have a clearer understanding of the important part *attention* plays in our relationships.

I found myself both laughing and crying. Connie's stories will hit home with you, I imagine, just as they did with me. There were times I felt she had been in *my* house, in *my* living room with *my* family. It was comforting to know that we all make the same mistakes.

This is one book you will want to keep close at hand to read over and over again. I recommend it for anyone wishing to improve an important relationship, not just those relationships dealing with children. Connie Podesta's 6-second secret has made a real difference in my life.

—Jennifer Fortenberry
Licensed Professional Counselor

Who Can Use This Book?

This book has been written so that young people as well as adults can read and enjoy it. I have tried to write the same way I would talk to you if you were here with me: from my heart with common sense—and a bit of humor.

I have received many letters, telephone calls, and e-mails from around the country. People of all ages have wanted to tell me how this book has helped them and how it has helped others in their lives.

Here are ways the book can be used by different individuals.

Students: Young people from fifth grade and up have read this book and shared it with their friends *and* parents. One junior high school student wrote, "Thank you for your book. My mom has never felt very good about herself, and it made me feel bad because I think she is a really neat person. I gave her your book, and we talked about it. She said if it would help me, she would work to like herself better."

Parents: We never know *everything* there is to know about our children. I try in the following pages to shed light on one aspect of growing up into secure, confident adults. Parents tell me it helps. One mother wrote, "I leave your book by the side of the bed. It's where I'm assured of peace and quiet away from the kids, and I can go read it when I need it the most."

Husbands and wives can also read it together, then ask their children to discuss it with them. Some stimulating conversations are bound to result!

Teachers (with students): Many teachers read the book aloud, or have students read it at home and then discuss it in class. The ideas and examples presented lend themselves to class discussions, particularly when students are encouraged to relate their own experiences. I've had many students write me with their own personal stories as a result.

Teachers (with parents): Often teachers need to meet with the parent(s) of a child who is struggling with self-esteem. And often it is difficult to explain to the parent what self-esteem is *without* the parent feeling defensive or at fault. In these cases, teachers send the book home with the child and ask that the parents read it before coming in for the teacher-parent conference. Parents then come in with ideas and suggestions of their own and truly participate in developing a plan of action.

Counselors: I used this book in my private practice with clients and have had many other counselors tell me they do the same. It can be used as supplementary reading for parents, couples, young people, and older clients. The principles outlined go hand in hand with concepts explored in group and family therapy.

School counselors, social workers, mental health counselors, drug and alcohol counselors—indeed anyone working with youth or with any individual who could benefit from increased self-esteem—can use the book to reinforce the message of the counseling program.

Health care personnel: In health care facilities through-out the country, this book can be found in education department libraries and gift shops. "Guest relations" pro-grams have used it to send the message that self-esteem is the foundation of treating others with dignity and respect.

Managers in the workplace: Skills that help us become better parents also help us become better managers. Indeed, family and work are both businesses. Each have budgets, departments, delegators and workers, rules and policies, and *problems.*

Acknowledgments

As I write this, I think of the Academy Awards ceremony. The stars seem to go on forever thanking people we've never heard of while we're saying, "OK, OK! Let's get on with the show."

Until this moment, I never realized that it wasn't important at all that 99 percent of the people watching didn't know or care about the recipients of the thank-yous and praise. It was only important to the people it was intended for.

So this is my personal page to tell the people special only to me:

Thank You

Thanks to my sister, Vicki—You have always been my friend as well as my sister. You are a talented speaker, actress, and songwriter, and I enjoyed writing my second book, *Life Would Be Easy If It Weren't for Other People,* with you. You've always been there to give me support in time of trouble, advice in time of frustration, and lots of great fun no matter what the time. I may be the older, but you are often the wiser.

Thanks to my friend, Jenny—We walked miles together in the hopes of attaining our youthful figures again. Instead, I gained five pounds and a friend who would listen, care enough to be honest, and laugh with me even when life wasn't funny.

Thanks to my daughters, Nicki and Marcie—I wish I had known the things in this book *before* you were born. Instead, the three of us learned the hard way—through trial and error—but always with love. Now it's your turn.

And the most special thank-you of all goes to you, my husband, Larry—Your support and encouragement to "go for it" have always been there—just like you. Please don't be fooled—even when I seem the most confident and sure of myself, I'm glancing over to make sure you're beside me.

About the Author

Connie Podesta is an international speaker, known for her entertaining and unforgettable performances. She is a licensed professional counselor, comedienne, actress, educator, playwright, songwriter, and radio/TV talk show host with more than twenty-five years' experience in all industries—corporate, health care, and education. Connie has addressed more than two million people throughout the world on key topics, including, "Life Would Be Easy If It Weren't for Other People," "How to Be the Person Successful Companies Fight to Keep," "If We're Going to Win This Race, We Need to Run in the Same Direction," and "Everyone Thinks They Can Do My Job, but Nobody Wants It" (a leadership keynote). She has authored three books, *Life Would Be Easy If It Weren't for Other People, How to Be the Person Successful Companies Fight to Keep,* and *Self-Esteem and the 6-Second Secret.*

*I dedicate this book to my parents,
Bill and Kathy Purvis,
who were always proud of even my
smallest accomplishments and accepted
my flaws without disappointment.*

*I would never have had the confidence
to pursue so many different paths in my life
if it were not for their constant message
that I was "OK," even when
I faltered and made mistakes.
That was their special gift to me—
a gift I try daily to pass on to my daughters,
Nicole and Marcie, and
my granddaughter, Jamie.*

If you're like me, there are a thousand things that need to be done right now that seem more important than reading this book. In fact, if you are really like me, this book has been sitting in your "read it later" pile waiting for the perfect time when everything is done and you can just relax and do something for yourself.

Have you even made it this far without the phone ringing, the kids crying, or UPS wanting your signature? If so, *great!* If not, I understand. After all, it took me two years to find the time to *write* this book.

Have you ever wondered how we all got so busy? And if it's worth the effort? I have. Sometimes I look at my children, who are growing up so quickly, and I wish I could start all over again. I'd nag less and hug more. I'd talk less and listen more. I'd react less and feel more. But most of all, I'd do everything I could to make them feel they were capable of achieving their most wonderful dreams.

Have you ever had those same thoughts?

If you have, then maybe we ought to do something about it. We can't start over—but we sure can start tomorrow. (That's not procrastinating—you need *today* to finish the book.)

So, take the phone off the hook and sit back in your favorite chair, because I'm going to tell you a secret. It's a secret about self-esteem and a 6-second miracle. It's a secret that can make life a lot happier. There is only one thing different about this secret—you can tell everyone you meet, because the sooner this secret is out, the better our world could be.

Right about now, you might be asking, "How come *she* knows this secret and I don't?" That's a strange thing too. When you finish this book, you are going to say:

1

"I knew that!"

And you did. But it's one of those secrets we just keep forgetting. That's why I decided to write this book—I never want to forget it again.

When I think of self-esteem, I get a bit sad. Sad because the idea is really so simple, but putting it into effect can be so hard. Sad because what I say out of love may be interpreted as criticism and I don't even realize it. Sad because some of the things I do out of a deep desire to raise my children to greater heights may be exactly what pulls them down.

If, after you've read these first two pages, I've touched any tiny chord, let's work on this together. Let's figure out this whole self-esteem bit once and for all, because that's the easy part. The hard part is reaching inside and taking a long, hard look at just how much we like ourselves before we dare to reach out to our children.

So, Just Exactly What Is Self-Esteem?

Self-esteem is currently a buzzword for everyone from the psychologist working with the family to the teacher in the classroom to the mom entering her three-year-old in preschool. We read about it in magazines, we hear about it at PTA meetings, and we can see how it affects those around us.

Professionals argue about the best way to instill self-esteem in our kids if it isn't there to begin with and how to raise it if it is. But self-esteem is not something we can raise or lower at will. Many books and articles have been written on the subject, but the arguments about self-esteem still rage.

When asked to define self-esteem, almost everyone answers in one of three ways:

1. Self-esteem is how we feel about ourselves.

2. Self-esteem is how much we like ourselves.

3. Self-esteem is the amount of confidence we have in ourselves.

I think to truly understand self-esteem, however, we must look deeper than those definitions. It is not sufficient to just like oneself, as evidenced by the fact that there are many people who like themselves so much that they are obnoxious and inconsiderate of others.

A report from the California Task Force to Promote Self-Esteem contains the following definition. I share this with you because it puts into words what many of us have been feeling—that the real issue of self-esteem has to do with how we treat others as much as it does with how we feel about ourselves. The definition reads:

> "Self-esteem is appreciating my own worth and importance and having the character to be accountable for myself and to act responsibly toward others."

What this means is that self-esteem is of little value if we do not use our good feelings to love, nurture, and encourage others around us.

No one denies that a healthy, solid sense of self-esteem is one of the most important gifts we can give a child. Everyone agrees that a child with high self-esteem is far less apt to use drugs, get in trouble with the law or at school, have inappropriate sexual relationships, or suffer from poor grades and unsatisfying peer group relationships.

So, if we know what self-esteem means and we all agree it is important . . .

What's the Problem?

The problem is that good definitions and honest intentions aren't enough.

Most parents believe that if they praise their kids regularly—*"Honey, I'm so-o-o proud of you. Why that's a beautiful picture!"*—and avoid put-downs—*"Shut up! How could you be so stupid?"*—it should be enough to keep the child's self-esteem in one piece.

Yet many parents who make a point of avoiding constant criticism and who use compliments and encouragement as much as possible still find themselves face to face with children they love dearly but who do not have much self-confidence.

To understand the "6-Second Secret" and put it into effect, you have to first understand and believe that the driving force behind us all (once our basic needs for food, shelter, and warmth are met) is the need for:

ATTENTION

I've yet to meet a person whose reactions, needs, thoughts, and actions are not centered around this desire for attention. We are a species that need other people. We all want more than anything to be loved, respected, admired, appreciated, and recognized as special human beings.

In fact, the complete absence of attention can destroy a child emotionally and, in some cases, physically. In *Dare to Discipline,* Dr. James Dobson tells us, "It has been known for several decades that an infant who is not loved, touched, or caressed will often die. Evidence of this fact was observed as early as the thirteenth century, when Frederick II conducted an experiment with fifty infants. He wanted to see what language the children would speak if they never had the opportunity to hear the spoken word. To accomplish this dubious research project, he assigned foster mothers to bathe and suckle the children, but forbade them to fondle, pet, or talk to their charges. The experiment failed because all fifty infants died" (Bantam Books, 1970, p. 33).

There is also a recorded experiment done by the Nazis during World War II. They took several babies and put half in one room and half in another. The temperatures in the rooms, the feeding schedules, and all other variables were the same.

The mothers in one room, however, were instructed to give the babies constant attention. So the mothers rocked them, held them, loved them, talked to them, and nurtured them. And, even in a concentration camp, these babies thrived! They gained weight, their cheeks were rosy, they smiled, they cooed.

The other babies were taken away from their mothers and given to caretakers who were instructed to give them no attention. They did feed them, but they averted their face when feeding them. They never made eye contact with the babies, never looked at them, never spoke to them, never picked them up, never touched them, never turned them over.

This last group of babies began losing weight and withdrawing. This is often referred to as "failure to thrive" or the Love Deprivation Theory. Slowly, these babies began to die.

The only variable in the care of these babies was attention. We are a species that will *die* without attention. Are you saying to yourself right now, "Well, I know attention is important, but I've never known anyone to really die from the lack of it."

Think about it. If people don't feel loved and appreciated by those around them, if they feel neglected, maybe they won't die physically, but they can make the choice to die in other, equally devastating ways. They can "die" emotionally through drugs, alcohol, depression, or withdrawal. And if they feel completely disconnected, they can contemplate or actually commit suicide.

For some reason, however, attention has gotten a bad rap lately. People say with disgust, "Oh, all they want is attention," as if wanting attention is automatically a bad thing.

I have heard parents of children who have attempted or threatened suicide say, "They're just trying to get attention."

You're darn right. That's what each and every one of us wants. It is not a weakness, it is not a sign of dependency— it is a wonderful, special quality of our *humanness*. So if we can finally resolve, with heads held high, that we each strive daily for attention, let's define what *attention* truly is:

Attention

is the

amount of time

and the

amount of energy

spent

in any given situation.

How do we decide whether our need for attention is being filled? By measuring the time and energy others spend when they are with us.

If I came home from work one day excited about what I had accomplished and said to my husband, "Larry, you won't believe what happened today," and he barely looked up from the paper and muttered, "Oh yeah, what?" I would begin to feel neglected.

If I continued to talk and he responded (still reading) with murmurs of, "Oh, that's nice, Honey," I would give up and stop sharing.

Why?

Because he's given me no time (minutes spent concentrating on me and nothing else) and no energy (eye contact, gestures, facial expressions, enthusiastic tone of voice).

In reality, if I come home bursting with news, I can count on Larry to say, "Just a minute." He'll go in the kitchen, fix us a cold drink, bring it in, sit back in his easy chair with a smile, and say, "Go for it; I'm ready to hear all about it."

Now I am having attention paid to me. He's given me his time (nothing else is going on except our conversation) and his energy (interest level, support, and concentration on me).

And boy, do I feel good!

Think about the last time someone really gave you his or her full attention, really concentrated on what you were saying. Didn't it feel good to you too?

Now think about the last time you really gave your *full* attention to your child. When my daughter was eight years old, she came into the kitchen where I was busy putting groceries away. She was trying to tell me something that had happened at school, and I was trying to get my chores done so I could finally sit down.

As she was speaking, I was giving her cursory glances and a few, "Oh, that's nice, Honey's." She finally said, "Mom, you're not listening." I stopped, looked at her, and said, "Oh, yes, I am."

Guiltily, I acted very interested for about one minute before I started sneaking groceries out of the bag, trying this time to be more careful and not take my eyes off her again.

Not to be fooled, she suddenly walked out of the room with one last statement that only a child with utter honesty can make:

"Forget it, Mom . . . you just don't listen all by itself anymore."

We all have so many things going on in our lives that it's hard to put them aside to spend quality time with our kids. There's another overused phrase, "quality time." Just what exactly does that mean?

Quality time

doesn't cost money.

You don't have to leave home.

It's simply those wonderful

windows of time when we

"listen all by itself."

❖❖

Listening without judging is one of the best ways we can give another person that needed attention.

I know some of you are wondering, "Well, just how much time do you mean? Thirty minutes, two hours, a full day?

That, I find, is different with each individual. And even within each individual, the need changes during different developmental stages, seasons, and even times of day. (A five-year-old, for example, may need lots of attention in the morning, a little after school, none right after dinner, and lots again around bedtime.)

It does seem that if the time is undivided and the energy level is high, we tend to feel good about the attention fairly quickly. If not, we will demand more attention shortly.

A good example is a parent at the pool with the kids. The child is yelling, "Watch me! Watch me!" Generally, we glance quickly up from the book we are reading or conversation we are having with friends and answer, "Oh, that's great, Honey," and turn immediately back to what we were doing.

This is not perceived as attention. *No time. No energy.* The child will usually escalate attempts to fill the void by yelling louder, crying harder, and trying some elaborate new trick. Kids are no fools—they can tell whether we are invested in them or simply brushing them off nicely.

We need to make a choice. We need to give attention in its true sense, leaving the book or friend, going to the side of the pool, watching with enthusiasm, laughing and talking awhile without interference.

Or we need to decide this is not the time to give attention and tell the child firmly, "I am going to read for the next half hour, and I need you to practice your swimming tricks by yourself. I am not going to look up every few minutes and watch. At 2:30, I'll put my book away and come into the water and you can show me everything you've practiced."

Children handle this sort of directness very well. It actually gives them a feeling of security because they know that, at a certain time, you will drop what you are doing and give them your full, undivided attention.

Wouldn't you rather have your spouse be honest and say, "Honey, I'm in the middle of the news, which I've been looking forward to watching, but as soon as it's over, I'll turn the TV off, and you can tell me everything that happened today without interruption."

Or would you rather hear, "Uh-huh, uh-huh, uh-huh," as he or she keeps one eye on the TV as you tell your big news? And you stand there knowing that thirty seconds later he or she won't be able to repeat a single word of what you said?

Most of us are willing to wait for good, quality attention rather than have people act as though they're interested when they're really not.

If we can all agree that what we want more than anything (after our basic needs are met) is attention, and if we
understand that the definition of attention is *time and
energy spent,* let's learn about the three ways to give
attention.

Every time you come in contact with someone, you
make a choice to give attention in one of these three ways:

---

1. Positive

2. Negative

3. Ignore
(No time,
No energy)

---

1. You can choose to treat people positively
through praise, encouragement, smiles, or hugs.

2. You can choose to treat people negatively
through anger, criticism, sarcasm, abuse, frowns,
or disapproving looks.

3. You can choose to ignore people and not give
them any feedback at all through silent treatment,
indifference, rejection, or neglect.

Keep in mind that everyone who comes in contact with you also chooses one of these three ways to give you attention.

Remember . . .

The worst thing we can do
to anyone wanting our attention
is to ignore him or her.

Lack of attention reduces our will to function, thrive, and even continue living.

One of the main things to understand about attention is:

Positive attention is what we crave,

but in its absence

we will seek negative attention

rather than be ignored.

Let's go over this message again, because we are hitting on the main reason children act in ways that cause us to react with negative attention.

1. We are born to seek and accept attention. We prefer that it be positive.

2. We can "die" or fail to thrive from not enough, or lack of, attention.

3. When positive attention is not available, we will seek negative attention rather than be ignored.

Some of you may be saying, "But I don't ignore or neglect my children!" I always thought the same until one afternoon. See if you recognize yourself in the following scenario:

I had just gotten home from a crazy, stressful day at work. With an armload of groceries, I walked in and knocked over the dog dish. I was trying to get dinner on the stove when the phone rang and a lady from the PTA reminded me about baking cookies for the fundraiser. Then a neighbor rang the doorbell, wanting a donation for the Humane Society. Meanwhile, I was trying to get clothes from the washer to the dryer so I'd have something clean to wear to aerobics class that night. Then my twelve-year-old walked in from school.

Being the "good mom" that I am, I asked a few "Good Mom" questions: "How was school? Did you have fun? Did you remember your book money?"

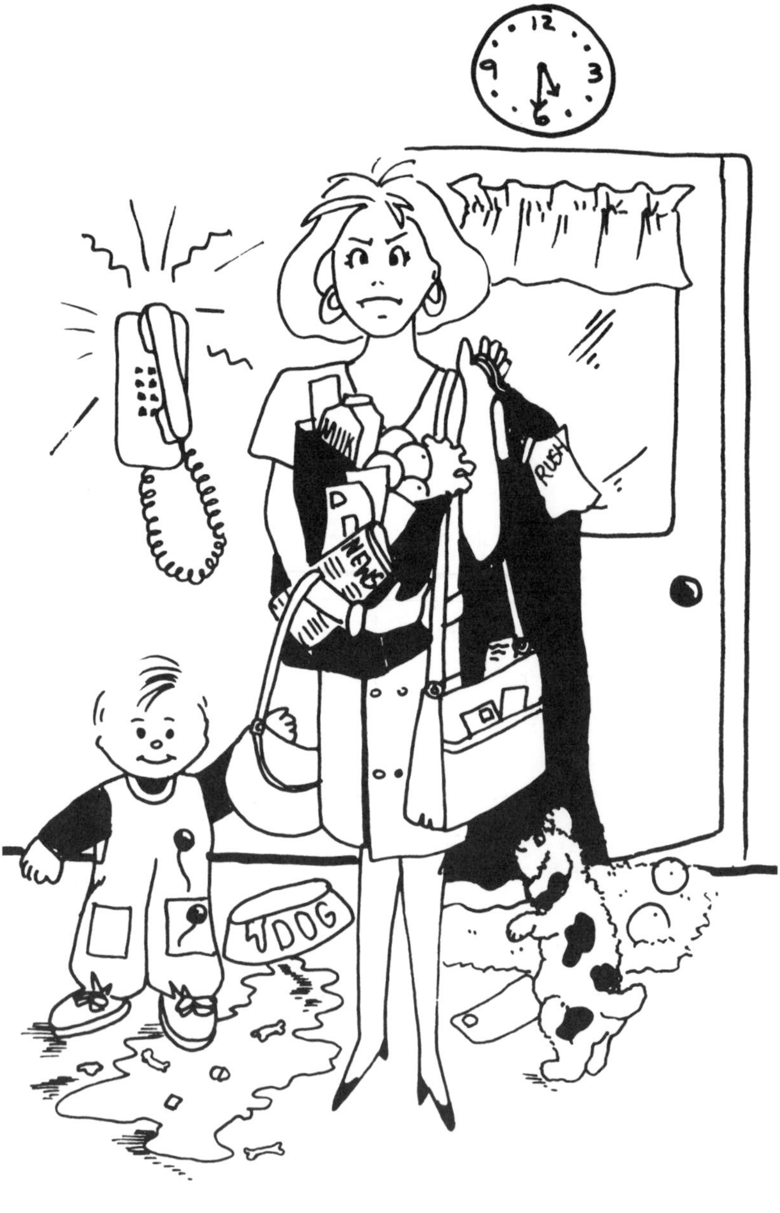
12
9
3
6
MILK
NEWS
RUSH
DOG

Then I did a little motherly nagging. . . . "Don't eat any junk; I'm fixing dinner. Pick up your books. You better get started on your homework if you expect to watch TV."

But then, after those few brief maternal proddings, what type of attention did my child get from me?

Positive? Negative? Ignore?

If you answered "Ignore," you're correct. After the interrogating and nagging (isn't that what moms are for?), I turned back to my busy routine. After all, I told myself, I'll have time *later* to sit and talk with her more.

Let's get this straight.

My child did everything a twelve-year-old could possibly do right. She made it to school on time, didn't talk back to any teachers, passed her test, didn't get suspended, didn't use any drugs or alcohol, didn't join any cults, came home on the bus with all the books she needed to study, walked in the house, and said in a bright, cheery voice, "Hi, Mom!"

Not a bad day for a twelve-year-old. In fact, she couldn't have done much more *right* if she had tried.

And what form of attention did she get as a reward for all her efforts? I ignored her. The worst of all!

The message we constantly give is when you do what you are supposed to do, I am very busy. But if you are in trouble, I will stop what I'm doing, I will stay home with you, I will do anything I have to do to fix you. I am never too busy to pay attention to you if you do something *great* or if you do something *terrible*. If, however, you are doing average—nothing extraordinary—I will probably focus on my own busy needs and won't notice you.

Therefore, if someone does not feel capable of performing extraordinarily well in order to get positive attention, he or she will soon learn ways to perform extraordinarily badly to get negative attention, which is preferable to being ignored or neglected. Remember:

We give most of our attention (time and energy) to extraordinary people . . .

those who are extraordinarily good

and

those who are extraordinarily bad.

It becomes apparent to most of us at an early age that the "average" person gets little attention at home, at school, or at work. After all, average people are simply doing what they are "supposed to do."

When are we going to learn that "doing what we are supposed to do" can be extraordinary in today's world of sneaky schemes, questionable ethics, and scary behavior?

Look at the following examples to see how we downplay the earnest contributions of the hard-working, "average" people around us:

Child: *"I know I forgot to clean the garage, but my room is all straightened up."*

Parent: *"But your room is supposed to be kept neat. That's your responsibility."*

— — — —

Employee: *"I wasn't able to complete all the extra work you gave me, but the quarterly reports are finished on time and sitting on your desk."*

Manager: *"So what? You always finish the quarterly reports on time. I really wanted you to give this new project your special attention."*

— — — —

Wife: *"I had a busy day and wasn't able to get the oil changed in the car. But I did pay the mortgage and get your prescription, and I'll get the oil changed tomorrow."*

Husband: *"That's just fine. If the car breaks down on the highway between now and then, I won't have any sympathy for you. I've told you a hundred times how impor-*

*tant it is to keep clean oil in the car, and
you don't pay any attention to me at all."*

So instead of the child feeling good about the room
he's cleaned, he's feeling bad about the garage he's overlooked. Instead of the employee feeling good about the
consistent performance she's turned in, she feels bad
about not being able to meet an emergency deadline.
Instead of the wife feeling good that she accomplished so
much in her busy day, including taking care of two errands
she thought were at least as important as the oil change,
she is chastising herself for not finding the time to cram
every possible errand into her schedule.

This technique of ignoring good behavior is a surefire
motivation killer, and *I can guarantee that if you don't
find time to give your "doing-what-you're-supposed-to-do"
child, employee, spouse consistent positive attention, they
will figure out a way to get consistent negative attention.*

Now I think you've been patient enough. Let's get to the secret. The secret is about compliments and praise and feeling good about ourselves. I need all of you to concentrate very hard and think of a compliment that someone paid you. (You can go back ten years, if necessary!) Was yours like one of these?

> **From a boss:** *"That was a great report. Keep up the good work."*
>
> **From a friend:** *"I love that outfit. It really looks good on you."*
>
> **From a child:** *"Thanks for letting me have Sara over. You're great."*
>
> **From a parent:** *"Good job on your test. You received a B. I'm really proud."*

Do you notice something about compliments?

They aren't very detailed. They don't take up much time to get out. In fact . . .

The average compliment takes 6 seconds or less to deliver.

That's not very long. It takes longer than that to zap leftovers in the microwave.

Aren't we wonderfully concise when we're giving compliments?

Isn't it amazing how little *time and energy* is spent telling people what they've done that's right and good? In other words, little *attention* is given when praising or paying compliments.

The average compliment

takes 6 seconds or less

to deliver.

Now ask yourself:

Are we just as capable of putting our concerns, gripes, criticisms, and irritations into 6 short seconds?

No way!

Think of a few criticisms you've delivered lately. For instance, when your child's room was messy, did you sound like this when you were telling her or him about it?

"Look at this room! It's an absolute pigsty! What's the matter with you? Your father and I raised you better than this! I am ashamed of this mess, and I'll tell you one thing, you're not budging out of this house this weekend unless this stuff is picked up, and I don't mean any halfway job either! When you grow up, you can keep your room anyway you like; but as long as you live in this house, you're going to live by our standards. Just who do you think you are, anyway? Do you think we have maid service? I'm not your slave! If you think I'm picking up this mess, you have another thought coming . . ."

and so on and so on and so on.

Gee, that took a lot longer than any of our compliments did, and that was actually the *Reader's Digest* condensed version of the typical "dirty room" tirade.

How about an employer who's disgruntled over a bungled assignment?

> *"George, get in here this instant and bring the Wellington file. What's the matter with you? Wellington just called, and we stand to lose the account because you forgot to include the buyout figures on the prospectus! How could you do such a stupid thing? I tell you, you are treading on thin ice. I don't care if Susan forgot to give you the figures . . . it was your responsibility to make sure they were included in the report, and you're the one who messed up. When the CEO hears what you've done, you'll really be in hot water!"*

Let's do one more. How about a working mom who forgot to pick up her son's soccer uniform?

> *"Mom, how could you forget?! Tomorrow is our team picture. You NEVER remember what needs to be done anymore! You're too busy worrying about your job."*

❖❖

Life is full of

6-second compliments

and

60-second complaints.

❖❖

Now here is the part you've all been breathlessly waiting for—the 6-Second Secret.

It's so simple, and yet it's one of the hardest things you'll ever learn to do. The secret can help you deal with children, co-workers, spouses, and in-laws (no kidding!). It can even help reduce stress.

Simply . . .

Reverse the process.

Try

60-second compliments

and

6-second complaints.

I told you it was simple. It's just so *hard* to do. We are so used to critiquing rather than complimenting that it's almost impossible to break old habits.

The secret is to simply spend more time complimenting and less time complaining, and I mean "time" as in length of time speaking, as in stop lecturing, as in be quiet, as in look for the good. Keep your criticisms under six seconds and expand your compliments to sixty seconds or so. It will sound something like this:

> *"Honey, I really appreciate the extra time you spend with the kids. I know how hard you work and how busy you are, but I can't overemphasize how important you are to them. I think that's one of the reasons our kids are so happy; they get to spend a lot of quality time with both of us. I just want to make sure you know how very much I love and appreciate you. You are a great parent."*

Wow! Doesn't that unsolicited compliment sound good? Wouldn't it make you feel good if it were directed at you? Wouldn't you go walking around about two feet off the floor if your spouse took the time to recognize something you were doing with a long, specific compliment?

How about boss to employee?

> *"Ellen, I noticed you've stayed late every night this week helping to get the Anderson project wrapped up. I just want to let you know how glad I am to have you on my team. You have contributed far more than you had to and shouldered more than your share of the burden on this assignment, and*

I appreciate it. You're a good team player, and you've shown real leadership skills."

Suddenly, we have an employee who is even more motivated than before, because she received the reward of positive attention. Somebody noticed she was doing something right and took the time to say something about it.

Here's a dad to a child:

"Son, I know your little sister gets on your nerves sometimes, and I want to let you know how much your mother and I appreciate it when you look after her for us. She really looks up to you, and it means a lot to her when you take her to the park or to get ice cream. And I know sometimes your friends make fun of you for dragging her along. I think it's wonderful the way you are committed to being the best big brother you can be, and I just want to let you know how much I love and appreciate you."

Are you beginning to see how this thing works?

Wasn't I right?

Isn't it incredibly simple? Are you sitting there nodding your head up and down and saying to yourself, "I knew that!"

I thought so.

I bet you're saying, "This isn't so difficult. Okay, I'll just elaborate a little more on the praising."

You're right. Praising isn't the difficult part. The real problem is in confining our criticisms and concerns to six seconds or less.

I love it! *Supposed* to lecture. The thing we hated the most as kids, we spend the most time doing as parents. Another reason for understanding the 6-second theory is that most people (and kids *are* people) tune us out after about six seconds of lecturing, nagging, and sermonizing. So why do we keep on doing it? Because it makes us feel better, at least for a little while. But we're really just wasting our time!

In other words:

Give attention

(time and energy)

to the positive

and do not give attention

(time and energy)

to the negative.

Now try expressing your concerns and needs using this technique:

1. Separate praise from concerns. Don't candy-coat honest gripes or needs.

2. Expand praise by describing behavior. Allow your voice, facial expression, and energy level to help deliver the message.

3. When you need to air a concern, deliver the message in six seconds or less. In six seconds, you can call the person by name, describe what is

needed, and give consequences of not following through.

4. Deliver these concerns without using much energy—eliminate screaming, crying, gesturing, and so on.

Here are some examples of how to express six-second concerns:

Parent to child: *"Shelly, I need you to put away your toys now. As soon as you're finished, you can go out and play with your friends."*

Teacher to student: *"Mark, I need you to work on your math problems instead of talking to Angela. Your schoolwork must be finished before you go to lunch."*

Friend to friend: *"I don't want to be late to class again tonight. If you're not here by 7:30, I'll go ahead and meet you there."*

As you become more and more comfortable with the 6-Second Secret and put it into practice more frequently, you will begin to notice a wonderful side effect. Even though you may have decided to try this approach to help your child or employee or friend, you will soon notice that you're feeling better too. More relaxed—*less stressed!*

Stress and burnout are both big buzzwords right now. There are lots of workshops, self-help books, and tapes available to help you deal with the pressure of modern life. They talk about eating right, getting enough sleep, exercising, taking deep breaths, and all of these indeed play an important part in keeping ourselves healthy and physi-cally fit.

But it is important to see these techniques for what they are—methods for treating the symptoms of stress more than for helping you identify and treat the causes of stress.

So what *does* cause stress? People are always calling me and asking me to do a workshop on "stress." I accept and deliver my "Dealing With Difficult People" workshop.

___

Why?

Because we are constantly

> *deciding which form of attention to pay to each person we meet (positive, negative, or ignore) in each separate situation while deciding how to react to the form of attention each person we meet has decided to give us (positive, negative, or ignore), which may affect which form of attention we decide to pay to that person the next time we see him or her.*

That's stressful even to read!

In other words, our biggest source of stress is *other people!* Or more accurately, our *reactions* to other people.

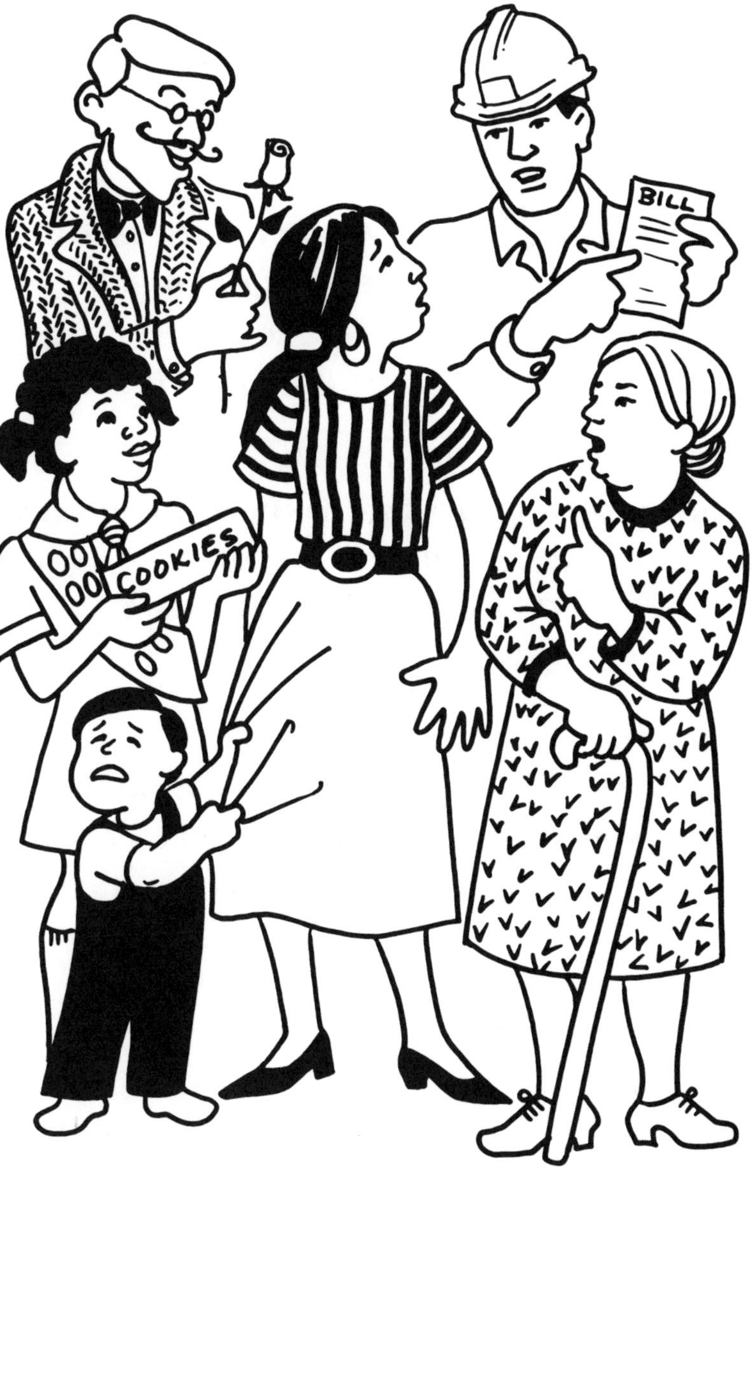
BILL
COOKIES

Let's go over that one more time:

Deciding which form of attention to pay each person we meet (positive, negative, or ignore) in each separate situation

while deciding how to react to the form of attention each person we meet has decided to give us (positive, negative, or ignore),

which may affect which form of attention we decide to pay to that person the next time we see him or her.

All the good eating, sleeping, and exercise in the world are not going to do the trick without a better understanding of how to communicate with the people around us.

The ability to communicate effectively helps reduce stress and allows us to feel more relaxed and peaceful.

❖❖

So what's all this got to do with self-esteem? When we feel stressed, we usually become impatient and intolerant. We feel overloaded and overwhelmed with the demands on us. We then tend to lecture, nag, and criticize those around us. When we feel time closing in, we don't take time for those special to us. We then feel guilty about being on edge, and that means we like ourselves a little bit less. And when we don't like ourselves, we aren't setting examples of high self-esteem to those around us.

And remember: As adults, our self-esteem must be intact for us to model confident behavior for our children. Therefore it is imperative that we confront the stress in our lives, because it is difficult to encourage feelings of good self-esteem in those around us when we are feeling angry, hostile, tired, and critical.

Our feelings about ourselves are reflected daily in our parenting techniques, so self-esteem is a family issue. We often hear self-esteem associated with words like "raise" or "lower." But self-esteem is not something we can raise like a flag on a pole for all to see.

We often read about self-esteem as if it were a gift we can give our children rather than an ongoing feeling present in the family. I'm not sure we ever become separated enough as parents from the issues surrounding our own self-esteem, the old tapes we play in our heads, our values, fears, and feelings about intimacy, to be able to "give" self-esteem to another human being.

Rather, we create perceptions of self-worth based on a myriad of feelings that exist within each family unit about life, values, fears, goals, judgments, and the capacity to love.

If self-esteem were indeed a gift, we would give it without reservation and have a generation of children secure, confident, and ready to face any crisis.

Instead, we have way too many children who turn to suicide at unbelievably young ages, who use drugs and alcohol to bolster their morale, and who join cults of various persuasions to feel loved and befriended.

Even within families who've been lucky enough to have children who make acceptable grades, stay away from addictions, and face life in a fairly positive manner, many parents will identify one child who does not have the confidence of the others.

In fact, many families experience a situation where one child is reasonably confident, does well in school, makes friends, and seems content with herself or himself and life, while a second child seems just the opposite. The parents are understandably confused. "How did this happen?" they ask. "Both children had the same opportunities, the same environment, and rules—the same amount of love."

Children are different. You probably noticed some of these differences from the moment yours were born. One liked to be held, another hated it. One child enjoyed all types of foods, the other only liked hamburger, pizza, and cereal. One wanted to please and was easy to discipline, the other almost dared you to set limits. You could tease one and she would laugh and tease back, the other would get her feelings hurt and pout.

It is important that we, as parents, feel good about ourselves and set examples for our children. But we must learn to accept the fact that some of our children may not *choose* to follow our examples or maybe they simply *can-*

not. Perhaps their individual personalities dictate that they see things in a different light, hear words and attach their own meaning, and struggle with feelings that we cannot control no matter how much we love them.

Often parents get hooked on, "Who is to blame for a child not having high self-esteem?" Perhaps no one. The uniqueness of each individual is just that—unique. Let's not worry about blame and fault. Let's concentrate more on acceptance.

First, we must accept that as parents most of us do the very best we can at each given moment, given the choices at that time.

Second, let's accept that each of our children will respond to us in a manner unique to him or her alone.

Third, let's accept that no matter what has happened in the past, today is a new day, and we can always learn more about ourselves and move ahead.

And fourth, let's accept that some children may not experience high self-esteem even though we have provided a loving, confident environment. And we may never know exactly why.

One tip, though. Once we identify children with low self-esteem, we tend to bombard them with questions: "Are you OK?" "What's wrong?" We may even say to them directly, "I wish you felt better about yourself." *Stop!* I think in our attempt to make them feel better about themselves, we instead continue to give messages that we think they are not OK.

Learning to accept some of these realities can be hard. But it may be even harder for some of us to forgive ourselves for some of the mistakes we have made. I can't think of a parent who doesn't regret some argument, angry outburst, or unfair punishment. We all play the "If I could do it again" tape. But we can't. The one emotion that can interfere with building self-esteem in ourselves and our children is:

GUILT

Guilt occurs when we spend more time worrying about the past than we do working toward a better future. When we feel guilty about what we have already done, we tend to try to make it up by giving in, saying yes when we should be saying no, buying material things, and accepting behavior that is not respectful.

Are you beginning to see why our own self-esteem must be in working order? We must accept ourselves, forgive mistakes we may have made, stop feeling guilty for what could have been, and *start today* to learn more about ourselves and others. And always remember the unfair rule of parenting:

The Unfair Rule of Parenting

*Some very **bad** parents have confident, successful children,*

and

*Some very **good** parents have difficult, frustrating children.*

Therefore we must work hard to establish and maintain our own self-esteem. Only then can we determine how we, as parents, contribute to our children's feelings about themselves. And to determine this, we must take a trip back to when we were young children.

We all begin our lives with the desire for positive attention. Children are born wanting to be loved, hugged, kissed, praised, and so on, and they soon learn what behaviors and traits will earn the positive attention they crave. There are five areas that seem to attract the most positive feedback from others, and they are:

Looks

Intelligence

Athletic ability

Talent

Personality

Let's look at these characteristics one by one:

Looks—It's no secret that our society admires the beautiful person. From the moment a child is put in the nursery, we ooh and aah over his or her beautiful features and have concerns about anything we consider less than perfect or different from what we expected. We count the fingers and toes. Just think how horrified we would be to find only nine, and yet, generally, that would have little effect on a child's performance. It's simply a sign of being less than perfect.

Attractive people seem to be assured of positive attention throughout life, sometimes without ever opening their mouths.

Intelligence—We test our kids earlier and earlier. We now have "preschool learning centers" and programs focused on those youngsters who are "intellectually above average." Therefore smart children are assured of some attention. They talk early, learn their ABCs, and can often be seen with a phone to their ear as young as eighteen months singing "Twinkle, Twinkle, Little Star" to Grandma amid squeals of joy from their parents.

Athletic ability—Children with athletic ability are assured of many forms of positive reinforcement through the years. They walk and ride bikes early and are often involved with team sports, which give tangible signs of positive recognition in the form of ribbons, trophies, and ceremonies.

Talent—The children who can draw, sing, dance, play an instrument, or exhibit other unusual skills generally receive extra attention. Their unique, special abilities are often envied by others who would like to be able to express themselves as well as the talented child.

Personality—These children have an ability to make others simply want to be with them—such as the charmer, the clown, the person whose presence is sought by others.

Most of us value one of these five traits more than the others. A former "Miss Cherry Blossom" may value looks, an accountant views intelligence and academic proficiency as the key to a profitable career, a retired pro quarterback revels in his son's athletic ability, a painter sees art as the highest calling one can have, and a sought-after keynote speaker believes personality is the one key to success.

What are you locked into? A good way to find out is to take the quick test below. By each trait, check whether you consider it: 1. Very important, 2. Somewhat important, or 3. Not essential for success.

	Very Important	*Somewhat Important*	*Not Essential for Success*
Looks	——	——	——
Intelligence	——	——	——
Athletic ability	——	——	——
Talent	——	——	——
Personality	——	——	——

The traits you checked as "Very Important" are the ones you are "keyed into." That means, for whatever reason, you have chosen to value these and will work hard to make sure your child values them above the others, too.

If you have a child born with a natural ability or desire to pursue the same direction as you, you may have a fairly comfortable relationship. But if you have a child who is not inherently successful in or desirous of developing the characteristics you value most, there is room for potential conflict, and the child's self-esteem may well be at stake.

For instance, John was very athletic in school and had decided to really push his two sons to excel in sports. He did this for many reasons: He enjoyed sports and has fond memories; he believes sports participation will give his sons a sense of sportsmanship and fair play and put them in contact with good, clean-cut kids; and sports stress the kind of strong, upright standards and morals he wants his sons to be exposed to. If one of his sons is athletic, John is likely to have a warm and mutually satisfying relationship with him. If, however, the other son is more oriented toward studies and not interested in sports, he may have a difficult relationship with his father. Not because he is not a "good" kid, but because he is not exactly the type of kid his father wanted to have.

Just keep in mind that these feelings are a result of John's own personal experiences; there are many other men who have a totally different view.

For example, Richard also played high school sports. He felt he was so busy practicing that it kept him from making the grades he wanted. He also was on a team that partied and drank, and he felt constant pressure to be "one of the guys." It was a stressful experience for Richard, so he has put athletic accomplishments at the bottom of his list in importance. He does not encourage his sons to participate in sports and, if they do, he makes sure they know sports should be at the bottom of their lists too. If their grades drop, he does not hesitate to blame their involvement in sports and ground them from practice. What happens to an athletically gifted son born to Richard? He may never receive much encouragement from his dad in the area he is most capable in.

Can you begin to see what happens to children who are born to parents who have preconceived notions of what their children both should and shouldn't do? As luck would have it, the odds are great that John will have a son who is studious and wants to play in the band, whereas Richard will father the next All-American quarterback. And in each case, the message to these boys could very well be:

> *"You are a disappointment . . . not quite what we, your parents, had in mind."*

Since I think real-life stories help us to understand things better, I'm going to share one with you—right from my very own home.

Those who know me best could take one look at the preceding list and know what I'm keyed into. Looks may be important when I'm on stage, but I'm very comfortable walking into the grocery in jogging clothes and without makeup. Intelligence—well, I hate to admit it, but I spent most of the nights before finals trying to average my grades and figure out what I needed to make on the exam to get a B in the course. Although I made good grades, I never felt the need to make straight A's. I am not particularly athletic, and I've tried every hobby in the world (sewing, cooking, art, and even needlepoint) without much luck.

Where does my energy and zest lie? You got it—*personality!* I majored in speech and drama. I love to socialize, talk to people, and get involved. I look forward to a good debate, am eager to share my innermost feelings, and enjoy group interaction.

So what type of messages did I give my daughter who was a bit shy, enjoyed her privacy, did not like to have deep discussions about personal feelings, and preferred to relate to people one-on-one rather than in large groups? Did I focus in on her strengths such as her good grades, her artistic talent, and her many blue ribbons in gymnastics? Oh, they all got their 6-second praises, but I really zoomed in on her need to be more outgoing. After all, she could already do all the other things on her own, so I needed to fill the role of a true mom and work on those areas that needed improvement. Isn't that what a "good" parent is supposed to do? Well, it sure is what we've been led to believe we should do.

So I went on a campaign to *fix her.* I had her answer the telephone to practice talking to more people, I sent her to pay the cashier at stores just for the experience of dealing with others, and I enrolled her in the school drama club.

One day when she was in the third grade, I came into her room and noticed her crying. She had to leave for her Brownie troop meeting soon, so I questioned her, and after considerable prodding she said she didn't want to go to the meeting. It was a show-and-tell day, and all the children were to bring special objects and tell the rest of the group why they were important to them. She, of course, was uncomfortable with this assignment and wanted to stay home.

How did I handle this?

I looked at her and said with conviction, "Honey, you are going to go to Brownies. You are just being silly. *You can't go through the rest of your life afraid to speak in front of other people.*"

And then I lovingly(?) pushed her out the door with tears in her eyes.

But what I told my daughter was a lie. There are many happy, successful men and women who are not comfortable sharing their innermost feelings with a large group of people. Why did I tell her what I did? Because I loved her, and I wanted her to be the best she could be. Yet what I really did was what many of us often do: I took *my* values and beliefs about what contributes to happiness and success and tried to instill them in her.

The problem with trying to induce self-esteem in others is that often what we say out of love and a deep desire to see our children adhere to our own personal values does not take into consideration their unique differences—differences that are not necessarily bad or good, just different. My main message to my child (who was successful in so many ways) was:

You're not OK, but I'm here to fix you.

Rather than accept our children as unique individuals with strengths of their own, we often set out to make them carbon copies of ourselves.

One day a friend quietly remarked, "It must be hard to have a mom who is as outgoing and verbal as you. I know

I'm rather shy, and I would always feel as though there were something wrong with me." Her words hit me hard. In my attempt to model self-esteem and give positive direction, could I instead be giving messages to my children that said, "If you're not like me, you're not OK"?

That afternoon I told my daughter I was wrong—that you *can* go through life without speaking on a personal level and opening up to every person you encounter. In fact, I told her that I was the unusual one. Most people hate public speaking. As I talked, I could see a smile begin to form and then she gave me a hug. That was a beginning— a beginning of a relationship where she could be accepted for who she was rather than who I wanted her to be.

It's never too late to learn important lessons. I'm glad I learned that one.

Perhaps unconditional love means that we as parents feel secure enough to allow our children to reach the potential they have chosen for themselves without feeling threatened, angry, or disappointed. Which brings up an interesting point. In my experience counseling children with low self-esteem, I find that the reaction they dread most from their parents is not anger, put-downs, or hostility, but *disappointment.* Watching their parents display feelings of disappointment through sad looks, sighs, comments, and even tears seems to do more to lower confidence than even loud, angry accusations.

Now you may be saying to yourself, Does this mean that my child must be successful in all five areas to be a confident, well-adjusted adult? *No!* The interesting thing is it has *nothing* to do with whether a child is born with these characteristics—it has to do with what children are *made to believe about themselves* from parents, preschool teachers, clergy, and any significant others in the first few years of life. That is why some people who are born with many handicaps seem to conquer the world, and some who appear to have everything are always unhappy and insecure. Many of us who are parents of physically perfect children cripple them with our unthinking criticisms of their ability or appearance.

It is possible to take a homely child and make her feel beautiful by showering her with love, affection, and lots of compliments. On the other hand, you can take a gorgeous child and quickly wreck her self-esteem by criticizing everything about her appearance and demeanor. Depending on what we say and do, we can have an average-looking child believing she is beautiful and worthwhile and a beautiful child believing she is ugly.

It is frightening to think we have that kind of power over a child's life.

I know a lovely woman who has a noticeable habit. Whenever she smiles, talks, or laughs, her hand automatically comes up to cover her teeth. Finally I asked her why she did it, and she told me her father had always made fun of the space between her teeth when she was an adolescent. He also said her gums showed too much when she smiled. Now here she is, many years and thousands of dollars worth of successful orthodontic work later, with a beautiful smile. But she is still covering her mouth with her hand when she laughs, because her father, who has been dead for seventeen years, convinced her that her smile was ugly and shouldn't be seen.

If this story strikes a chord with you, stop and think about what you are telling your children every day. Are you sending them messages that can damage their self-esteem, even though those messages were meant to be loving and encouraging?

As parents, we're so into issues of control—when, where, and how our children do things. We tend to forget that the most important thing we have to control is ourselves and our constant need to improve our children or remold them into something more pleasing to us.

"What now? You're telling me I'm not supposed to want more for my child?"

No, but in our attempts to improve, change, or redirect our children, what do they really hear? Now you may be saying, "But does this mean I shouldn't push my children to be the best they can be?" Maybe the bottom line is Who should decide what is the best? And can we, as parents, always be sure that those traits we value do indeed ensure happiness and success for everyone?

My next book should be titled *If We Talked to Our Friends the Way We Talk to Our Kids, We Wouldn't Have Any Friends*. I've learned that if I'm unsure how something might be perceived by my child, then I should test it out on another adult.

Let's take an ordinary parent pep talk and see how it sounds. Jennifer just came home with a report card with one A, two B's, and one C. The typical family scenario goes like this:

> *"Honey, this is really good, but what happened with this C? I know you can do better. Daddy and I are willing to help in any way. There's a great tutor on the next block, or I could help you after school. Maybe your friend Sara could come and study here; she's always done so well in math. We love you, and anything we can do to help, you just let us know!"*

Sound good?

Maybe it would help you sort out your feelings if we took the same kind of "loving lecture" we usually dump on our kids in the guise of improving them and changed the players to a husband and wife and a boss and an employee. As you are reading these little scenarios, try to put yourself in the place of the person being "talked to" and try to get in touch with how the conversations would make you feel if they were directed at you.

Wife to husband: *"Honey, I know you could get a better raise if you tried harder. How about taking some classes and brushing up on your skills? Maybe you could talk to our neighbor Bill—he's an excellent salesman*

*and might have some new ideas for you.
There's a great new book out that might
help you. I know you're capable of working
harder to get that raise next year. I'll be glad
to help any way I can. I know you can improve, and I just want you to know I'm with
you all the way."*

How do you think this husband feels right now? Not
very good, I imagine!

Here's another example:

Boss to employee: *"David, I know you're capable of doing better. I encourage and support you. Just tell me what you need. I know
from your resume that you have excellent
skills and qualifications. Do you need another secretary to help you get your work
out on time? Do you want to work with Sally
a few days and see how she organizes her
workload? Is your mind on other problems?
If so, we have a counselor on staff you
could see. I'll be glad to help any way I can.
I know you can improve, and I just want
you to know I'm with you all the way."*

Do you have any doubts about the real message?
Although it's couched in words of praise, people on the
receiving end of such comments don't feel praised—they
feel bad. The message they are hearing is, "You're not OK,
but I can fix you, so listen to me."

Do you think any of the people in these three examples feels better now than they did before they were
"encouraged"? Does the child want to rush to her desk and
open her books and start studying or would she rather

escape outside to play with her friends? Does the husband want to start putting in overtime and skipping lunch to impress his wife and his boss or would he rather turn on the TV and "tune out" the problem altogether? Does the employee feel like trying harder or not trying at all?

If you're not convinced yet, try this one:

> **Child to mom:** *"Mom, I know you could be a really good mother if you tried. You're smart and pretty. I know if you just put your mind to it, you could be a wonderful mom. I've heard there's a parenting class at the YMCA, and I brought you an application. Johnny's mom said she'd be glad to talk to you. She's a great mom and has raised four super kids. I just want you to know I love you, and I know that with a little work, you can be a super mom too!"*

Dig deep down inside. How would you feel after such a "chat"?

Bad? Why? Your child was so positive and so-o-o-o encouraging. But wouldn't most moms, husbands, employees, bosses, and so on be feeling . . .

hurt, angry, disappointed, confused?

Can you think of any example where being told you are capable of doing better would make you feel good? Think again about what you heard in our examples. You heard "praise" that sounded like criticism and delivered a negative message:

"You are NOT smart, competent, capable, caring, ambitious . . ."

In other words . . .

"You Are Not OK. You Need Fixing."

Do you see where the confusion comes in, and why our children tune us out after awhile? They start wondering how many other things we think are wrong with them.

We all know we should avoid name calling, hollering, and put-downs when dealing with our kids. We've also been taught to expect that if we do avoid these bad practices, our children will emerge from adolescence with their self-esteem pretty much intact. But how many other ways do we compromise our children's self-esteem with our misguided good intentions?

Let's look at another technique that we generally view as "positive encouragement."

Have you ever told your child, "But, Honey, you have so much potential!" as if by not doing or achieving exactly whatever it is we want, children are falling short of the mark.

Let's take a serious look at this thing called *potential.* How is potential determined?

Our children are tested early. These scores plus input from early childhood teachers are blended with our own beliefs about each of our children's capabilities. We add to this our own experiences and frustrations (things we love doing as well as things we wish we had done) and top it off with a dash of sincere desire to see each child "happy" (according, of course, to our own definition of "happy"). Mix this together and you have the age-old recipe for . . .

"Full Potential"

Let me ask you before we proceed any farther—

Do you have your Ph.D.? Well, why not? You're too busy? That reason is not good enough. You need to make the time to better yourself if you want to be successful. If you would just set your priorities, you could find the time.

Do you water-ski? You don't? What's the matter? You're afraid of water? Everyone else around here water-skis. Well, you can't go through life being afraid. If you really want to be the best you can be, you'll work on conquering your fears.

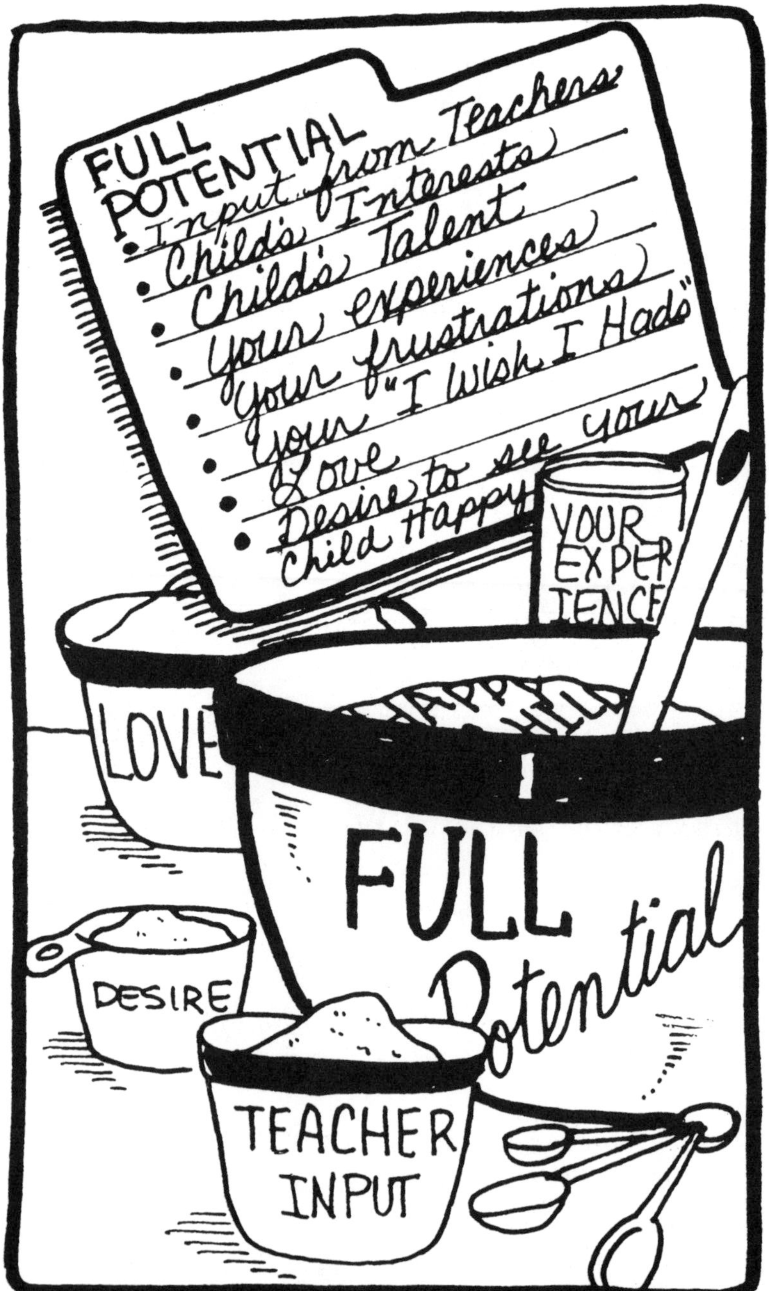
FULL POTENTIAL
• Input from Teachers
• Child's Interests
• Child's Talent
• Your experiences
• Your frustrations
• Your "I Wish I Hads"
• Love
• Desire to see your Child Happy
YOUR EXPERIENCE
LOVE
FULL Potential
DESIRE
TEACHER INPUT

Have you read all the classics? Why not? Because it sounds boring? Well, you can't expect to just have fun all the time. You need to be well read.

Before any of you ever again accuse someone of not reaching his or her full potential, ask yourself just one question:

Are you doing everything at this moment in your life that you are potentially capable of doing?

I know I'm not, and you probably aren't either, and that's OK.

But if it's OK for us adults to make choices—to decide we're too tired, busy, afraid, or uninterested to pursue certain goals—how come it's not sometimes OK for our kids too?

I realize some of you are saying right now, "But wait a minute, Connie. Do you mean that our kids should be given free rein to make any choices they want?"

No, certainly not. We need to set overall expectations and help our children meet those expectations and be the best they can be. I *am* suggesting, however, that we realize that achieving one's full potential twenty-four hours a day, seven days a week, is a mighty awesome expectation.

Children's lives change: divorce, health, moving, death, and physical development, to name just a few factors.

Here's another way of thinking about all this. How would you like someone else to decide what you are capable of doing and then demand that you reach this standard for the next fifteen to twenty years without regard to any crisis or changes that might occur during that period? Or even more important, without regard to your own perception of yourself and your desires and capabilities?

An example comes to mind:

Sue and Tom are newlyweds. Sue wants very much to please Tom, and Tom feels the same way about Sue. Sue is excited about their new apartment and loves to come right home after work and straighten things up so it's perfect for Tom when he gets home a half hour later. She also is anxious to try all her new recipes and cooks five-course dinners and puts fresh flowers on the table every night.

Meanwhile, Tom is eager too. He leaves work right on time because he wants to get home to Sue. He loves walking in right at 5:00. He gives her a big hug and kiss and immediately offers to help with dinner.

What if they each prepared a "full potential" standard for each other now that they know what each is "capable" of?

Sue would always expect Tom to:

1. Be home right at 5:00 every night

2. Always help with dinner

3. Hug her and kiss her fervently the moment he walks in the door

Every night, Tom would expect:

1. Sue to always be the one to start dinner

2. A spotlessly clean house whenever he steps through the door

3. A hug and kiss equal in ardor to the one he delivers

Are these realistic standards? Or have these two folks taken honeymoon behavior and mistakenly held it up as the standard by which they'll judge each other from now on?

Isn't it silly? Shouldn't people be free to bend and change with circumstance? No matter how much in love Sue and Tom are, eventually Sue is going to want to pop a frozen pizza in the microwave and let the newspapers sit on the chair a little longer, and Tom is going to want to slump in a chair, grab the remote control, and relax before he kisses Sue hello.

It's just human nature.

Now think about this: By the time their child enters first grade, most parents have already determined exactly what that child is capable of (straight A's and musically talented, but shy; C average, but outgoing and a great athlete; and so on). And generally they stick with their expectations all the way through their child's school years.

Twelve years of life! That is awesome when you think of the amount of change people go through between six and eighteen. They grow a couple of feet and gain sixty to eighty pounds in that period. I think it's a pretty safe assumption that as children's bodies grow and change, their skills, talents, abilities, and needs are growing and changing also.

How many of us are performing in the same manner, using the same criteria we were twelve years ago? If you were to look back at the past decade of your life, you would see periods of "brilliance" and "stupidity," flashes of creativity and utter dullness, and pockets of cooperation and old-fashioned stubbornness. And that's normal. We allow ourselves to grow and adapt to the changing conditions of our lives. In fact, we are usually not concerned, on a day-to-day basis, with reaching our "full potential," but rather with coping as best we can with the demands life is making on us at that time.

Then don't you think our children—who are worried about being accepted, making friends, studying, pleasing teachers and parents, and changing from children to adults—deserve the option to not always achieve their full potential (once in awhile)? The question is, can we be trusting enough as parents to let our children be less than perfect, just as we are less than perfect?

Along about now, some of you are probably asking, "Does this mean I can't encourage my children and tell them how capable I think they are?"

Absolutely not!

What it really boils down to is this:

❖❖

We talk too much

to *our children*

at *our children*

about *our children*

instead of

with *our children.*

❖❖

When we talk *with* an adult, we listen as much as we speak. We get the facts, figure out how the other person feels, and use this information to have a conversation. We have learned not to jump in and offer advice or opinions until we assess the situation, so we won't put our foot in our mouth.

For example, let's say you stopped by a friend's house and she had just had her dining room wallpapered. As you walked into the room, you noticed it was a terrible job—the stripes didn't match, the seams were uneven, and so on.

What would you say? Most of us would keep quiet until she spoke because we'd want to know how she felt. If she hated the way the wallpaper was hung, you would then jump right in to agree, "Boy, are you right! Yes, you do deserve to get your money back! It looks terrible!"

But if she really bubbled over with joy about how pretty the dining room looked, how pleased she was, and what did you think . . . isn't that a different story?

Some of you might simply agree that it looked lovely. Others who are more honest would offer comments about how it "might" have been put up a bit straighter, but I don't think many people would come right out and say, "It looks terrible! What a rip-off!"

But with our children, in the name of "encouragement," we often jump in without assessing how they feel first. Shouldn't our kids get as much consideration as our friends, and are we really so sure our child can do better? Did we ask?

Does this sound familiar?

> *"I want to know just how it is you came to get this C, and I don't want any stories or excuses. What earthly reason can there be for a C on the report card of someone as smart as you?"*

This does *not* count as assessing the child's feelings about his or her own performance. Simply take the report card, fix a snack, sit down with your child and say,

"Since this is your report card and your grades, why don't you tell me a little about each class? I know there are a lot of things that make up each final grade. I'm really interested how you're feeling about school and your progress."

And then listen.

Without disapproving looks, gulps, or rolled eyes. Remember, children seem to be affected by signs of disappointment as much, if not more than, by outright displays of anger and frustration. In my experience, they often interpret their parents' anger as being mad at something they *did,* but think that expressions of hurt or disappointment have to do with who they are *inside*—the kind of person they are.

The following are good guidelines when talking to people about their performance. If you follow these steps, "encouragement" will be perceived as positive and leave the recipients with a good feeling:

1. Assess the situation. See how the other people feel about the matter at hand. Allow them to talk first and do not set the stage with stares, frowns, sighs, and so on.

2. If they are disappointed with their performance, see if they have any ideas of their own about how they can improve. They are far more likely to improve performance if it is their idea rather than yours.

3. If they are content with their performance, find out why. Check to see if they realize the natural consequences of their actions. Are they willing to deal with the consequences?

4. Be a facilitator, not a dictator. If it is your idea, they may have little incentive to see it work. After all, it will be your idea that fails, not theirs.

The best encouragement is when we are supporting other people's ideas, goals, and beliefs about themselves, not when we are *telling* them what we expect.

Now that we've explored the area of "encouragement," let's take a look at ways we communicate our joy, pride, appreciation, love, respect, and thanks to those we care about (otherwise known as "positive reinforcement").

One problem with feedback is that often we don't separate our criticism and concerns from our praise; we weave them together, and as a result our message is confusing.

Therefore our compliments and attempts to encourage our children or others in our lives are not always perceived the way we intend them. Sometimes we "sandwich" our concerns between positive statements or simply add the infamous "but" after a compliment, giving in to temptation to throw in at least one area that could stand improvement. Even though the "sandwiching" approach is often taught in communication classes, I believe it is a confusing and manipulative technique that should be avoided.

We can praise our kids, and we can point out areas of concern, but let's skip the candy coating and stop throwing in praise to soften the blow of an honest gripe. Our kids are so used to hearing us buffer our criticisms with halfhearted praise that when we do have a real compliment to pay, they may not hear it.

Why are so many parents afraid to offer honest, negative feedback? Because we've read so much about the importance of not criticizing our children too harshly, many parents are afraid to say anything negative to the little darlings at all. But of course, kids and their parents are going to have conflicts, so we've gotten into the habit of giving a "spoonful of sugar to help the medicine go down," as they say in *Mary Poppins*. And kids see right through it.

If you are going to praise your children, praise them, period. Stop adding the "but." Get your kids out of the habit of waiting for the other shoe to drop, and they will learn to listen better to what you're actually saying.

If you are going to express need or concern, then do it! A child can handle honest feedback without injury if it is fair, concise, and *brief!*

For example, about the report card with the one C grade:

> **Praise:** *"An A in science. Super! That is a difficult course. You must have worked hard. I was really impressed with your science project and thrilled when you won that second-place ribbon. It must have made you feel proud to know the judges recognized how very hard you worked. I know your father and I are certainly proud of you."*

> **Praise:** *"I like seeing this A in math. It shows you were organized and studied hard. I never did*

well in math, and I admire the way you seem to grasp math concepts so well."

Praise: *"This B shows a great deal of improvement. I know writing isn't your thing, but I've been really pleased at how you worked to improve your writing skills. You've come a long way. I know you tried hard to pull your grade up."*

Concern: *"The C is lower than you usually get in English. What's up?"*

Then listen. Really listen! And notice how much time was spent on praise versus concern. Also notice the concern was the last thing to be discussed. (A good rule of thumb is to discuss each grade in the order it appears on the report card.) Your message is that you are equally interested in each class and not focusing just on the bad.

Let's avoid the typical parental response:

"This is a great report card, but why did you get a C in math? Are you doing your homework? Do you need help? Should I meet with the teacher? Your dad and I always did well in math, so I know you can too. You certainly have the potential. What's your problem?"

The good grades are barely recognized before the "but" appeared. Emphasis was solely on the negative.

Building our children's self-esteem is such an important job for parents. It is a task that demands our full attention. In today's world, with its many temptations, we could not equip our children better than to instill in them feelings of self-worth and self-confidence.

Even though a child's self-perception is formed very early in life, the major impact of low self-esteem may not manifest until adolescence (junior and senior high school). It is at this point that friends and peers are of the utmost importance to the child. We, as parents, are generally pushing for the child to start getting involved in the "good" groups and clubs in school—sports, student council, yearbook, chorus, band, cheerleading, and so on.

How does self-esteem play a role here? If you think about the five areas we discussed—*looks, intelligence, talent, athletic ability, and personality*—it is almost impossible for children to become part of any of the groups, clubs, or organizations that parents want for them without feeling secure in two or three of these areas. In other words, there are prerequisites to becoming part of the groups we would like to have our children belong to. Prerequisites in the eyes of those electing, judging, or inviting them to belong—and in the eyes of the child.

Most children will not run in an election, try out for a team, or apply for a club if they do not feel they have an excellent chance of making it. Kids do not like rejection any more than we adults.

So what attracts our children with low self-esteem who have the same need to belong and be part of the peer system? Well, ask yourself What groups have no prerequisites? What kids seem to care less about looks, intelligence, and athletic ability? Where is personality not a necessity and talent overlooked? How about the young people involved in using and selling drugs? Drinking? Those involved in early and promiscuous sex? Cults?

Let there be no doubt about it—our children will find a group that will accept them just as they are.

Is self-esteem important? You bet! It is what makes kids confident to surround themselves with friends and peers who also feel good about themselves. And it reduces the need to get involved with drugs, alcohol, and other not-so-wonderful situations.

We hope our kids will "just say no," but I have seen the children say "yes" in order to be part of a less-than-desirable group as an alternative to being ignored and alone. The drug, drink, or sexual act may be secondary to the foremost need—*attention*. If that's the case, helping our kids feel good about themselves will contribute more to the war on substance abuse than anything else.

I could not finish this book without telling a story about a special young man named Phillip. His eloquent words remind me daily of the role we play in a child's life.

Phillip was thirteen when his parents brought him to me for counseling. He had been diagnosed as depressed, uncommunicative, and suffering from low self-esteem.

He was indeed hard to talk to, but I found he was an avid writer of both fiction and poetry. I asked if he would like to write to me and express how he was feeling.

The next week, he came to see me with two sheets of paper. One was a sheet of filler paper, and the other was a sheet of lovely, parchment stationery.

At the top of the filler paper, he wrote, "Read me first."

Dear Mrs. Podesta,

I feel like this sheet of filler paper. You can buy 500 or 1,000 sheets at any drugstore or dime store. It's inexpensive. It's used for rough drafts and to write down things that aren't important. No one thinks about what they're going to write or say; they don't care about what utensil they're going to use; they just write down anything that comes to mind. If they make a mistake, they just cross it out or erase it. If they accidentally make a hole, they just wad it up and throw it in the garbage because they can always get another sheet of filler paper.

On the beautiful stationery with india ink in flowing calligraphy, Phillip had written:

What I want to feel like is this sheet of stationery. This sheet of stationery is so expensive, so special, that no one would use it for a rough draft. They take it out carefully, set it on the desk. Then they stand back and agonize over everything they are going to put on it. They know it is so special that they would never want to put anything on it that wasn't just right. They know that everything written on the stationery will be there forever and ever.

Phillip has given us a perfect description of self-esteem: feeling that you are worth something and that you matter. Our children deserve to feel like the finest parchment stationery. What we do and say directly affects the way they feel about themselves not only today, but for the rest of their lives.

So Is That It?
Is the Secret Finally Out?

Yes, but the hardest part is still ahead—making it work. And the reason it's so hard is that our own self-esteem must be intact. Our children watch us as though we were in a play, and in time they will become the actors and repeat the same performance for their children. A great deal of our children's self-esteem will simply come from modeling our confident behavior, our ability to take care of and treat ourselves respectfully, and our own sense of inner worth.

I have attempted in this book to give you some insight and ideas that might help you pursue the goal of helping others feel better about themselves. But there is nothing written or documented that can "give" another person a true sense of self-worth. We can, however, "give" the gift of self-respect to ourselves. In the end, we must all decide for ourselves which messages we will take to heart and which ones we will discard and just how much we like and respect our own being.

There is no better gift to give a child than an adult who has—and who shows through day-in and day-out behavior—a strong sense of dignity and self-esteem.

And that is the true secret!

Useful Materials

Connie Podesta has a variety of useful materials such as books, audiotapes, and videotapes available for sale. In these items you will find humor, as well as solid content, to help you in your professional and personal life. For more information on how to obtain these items, please check her Web site:

www.conniepodesta.com.

Workshops, Presentations, and Keynote Speeches

Connie is available as a dynamic and engaging speaker. She has created a dramatic series of presentations designed to explore the skills needed to successfully face life's challenges, provide quality service, respect others, believe in one's self, work in a team, establish solid family relationships, and develop positive attitudes.

Connie works with clients to customize her programs to meet individual organizations' specific needs. For topic fees or a complete information packet, please check her Web site.

CORWIN
PRESS

The Corwin Press logo—a raven striding across an open book—represents the happy union of courage and learning. We are a professional-level publisher of books and journals for K–12 educators, and we are committed to creating and providing resources that embody these qualities. Corwin's motto is "Success for All Learners."